SKY GAZER

ALAN HOLDER

ANAPHORA LITERARY PRESS

AUGUSTA, GEORGIA

ANAPHORA LITERARY PRESS
2419 Southdale Drive
Hephzibah, GA 30815
http://anaphoraliterary.com

Book design by Anna Faktorovich, Ph.D.

Cover Image: "Sea" by Lionel Walden.

Published in 2016 by Anaphora Literary Press

Sky Gazer
Alan Holder—1st edition.

Print ISBN-13: 978-1-68114-207-4
ISBN-10: 1-681142-07-4
EBook ISBN-13: 978-1-68114-208-1
ISBN-10: 1681142082

Library of Congress Control Number: 2015915803

SKY GAZER

ALAN HOLDER

for Rosanna,
once more

CONTENTS

OTHER BOOKS BY ALAN HOLDER

Three Voyagers in Search of Europe: A Study of Henry James, Ezra Pound, and T.S. Eliot
A.R. Ammons
The Imagined Past: Portrayals of Our History in Modern American Literature
Rethinking Meter: A New Approach to the Verse Line

Voices Against Silence (poems)

Chapbooks

Opened: A Mourning Sequence
Aging Head in the Clouds

ECONOMY MOTEL

To Whatever Reader Happens Along

Someday you may have to eat your words—
that's none of my business.
But whatever the case, for now
I hope you'll eat mine,
that is, stick them in your mouth
as they come to you, one by one,
in these tidy packages of lines,
then emit them (silent reading be damned),
turning yourself into something
being played by me, but not as a stooge,
no, more as a violin or piano,
no, not that either, because an instrument,
even if a Strad or a Steinway,
is still just a thing, hopelessly cut off
from the feeling being driven through it,
whereas I take you (as I take myself)
to be a creature of feeling, for,
if you're not that, what are you?

So forget the instrument bit
and try this: let your mouth
be that rare thing, a full-service
economy motel, offering tongue, lips,
teeth, palate, vocal chords, to words
otherwise homeless—my gratitude shall be your pay.

IN DEFENSE OF CRYING

We need more crying—
Chuck Klosterman on the subject
of canned laughter.

Exactly.

My pusher (pharmaco-psychiatrist to you)
is disturbed when I tell him I cry
frequently—he takes it as a sign
of depression. Still, I often cry
even when observing happy things—
reconciliations, declarations of love
(as in Hollywood romantic comedies).

But whether the occasion is happy
or sad, I welcome the seizure of sobs
welling up from a deep cistern
ordinarily covered over, ignored.

Was there ever such a thing as a *bad* cry?
So, world, keep your pills, and confine
your canning to sardines.

STEVENS CAN KEEP HIS CONNOISSEUR OF CHAOS

I'd rather be a connoisseur of clouds
(for which he himself had a soft spot),
especially those traversing wide-open,
unobstructed skies. But how can I
become an expert in glorious ephemera
inexorably slipping from one shape,
one coloration, to another, as at sunset?
Are clouds, then, just one more instance of chaos,
chaos in slow motion, and have I merely
circled back to Stevens?

A fresh start—let me drop the notion
of cloud connoisseurship, and settle
simply for being cloud-struck, as avid
in looking at what moisture and sun
and wind can do, as any astronomer
gazing up at his starry, starry night.

SKY AT 8:45 p.m.

Not the sunset portion of it, not at all,
but rather its counterpart in the east,
white-fringed at the top, the rest showing
a range of shades from blue to purple,
the base of it, above the houses,
a huge bruise, menacing and gorgeous,
the whole arrangement drifting slowly,
strangely, to the north, quickly fading
to one more ending, mocking any wish
that this gratuitous beauty would freeze
in place, if only for half an hour, making
for something more wonderful than the sun
obeying the commandment to stand still.

SKIN-DEEP

A newly-split tree (wind? lightning?)
shows us what it has been hiding
behind dirty-brown, scaly bark: fresh, creamy,
yellow-white wood, slightly striated.

Opened up, by shell or scalpel,
we can offer the viewer only a tangle
of tissues and throbbing guts, brilliantly
striving to keep us alive,
but nothing we want to look at.

Why is "skin-deep" synonymous
with "superficial"? Blessings
on our largest organ, this profound,
faithful disguise—I'll take any skin
over what lies beneath it.

SKY WINDOW

After a slight release of rain,
this early evening sky, worthy
of Turner, cries out to be looked at,
turbulent, fermenting grays, light
and dark, packing the dome, but
halfway up, to the east, a roughly
oval light-blue clearing appears—
impossible to say which is more
wonderful, this small, luminous window
or the massive Baroque framing of it.

COUNTERING CHAOS

Whenever I find a library book mis-shelved,
I pluck it out and put it in its rightful place,
and if I klutzily knock a piece of fruit
to the floor in a market, I pick it up
and put it back in the appropriate pile
(giving it a swift, surreptitious swipe
on my clothes to clean it), and I never
leave ill-fitting clothes in the dressing room,
but return them to the exact rack
where I found them.

Why do I do this, you might ask—why why?
To do my bit in the battle against Chaos,
join the struggle, in my small way,
to overcome the monarch pictured
by Milton as companioned by Night,
Chance, Tumult and Confusion,
or, if you need a more modern way
of looking at it, to stand up to the Second Law
of Thermodynamics, which has things
tending toward homogeneity, uniformity,
all entities losing their integrity
and distinctive location, everything
being shmooshed together
to form a featureless stew,
the Library of Congress shelving system
shot to hell, apples and oranges
hopelessly mixed together, no such thing
as finding 34"x30" pants—is that what you want?

NOT A JAR IN TENNESSEE

I placed a jar in Tennessee
                    —Wallace Stevens

Carelessly nudged over counter-edge,
the newly-washed glass, just a second
before a beautiful, useful cylinder,
now instantly gripped by gravity, explodes
into countless, jagged, shining
fragments, each fit only
for drawing blood from the hand
that would gather it up,
each a gleaming illustration of a law
of creation: anything made sits on
the brink of instant unmaking.

TWO STONES

My massive gold ring was first
set with a lapis lazuli stone,
precisely, diagonally bisected
by a thin, inserted gold strip.

Careless movements over time
cracking the stone, the ring,
unable to hold it any longer,
is now re-set with lapis,
but this specimen, sans gold strip,
has its deep blue sprinkled
with intrinsic, minuscule, gold
droplets, making for a little heaven.

We need both—the elegant
symmetry of the first,
everything in its place,
the product of skill, control,
conscious design—
and the random scattering
of the second, gift of Nature's
tossed-off, tiny radiance.

THE BABES IN THE WOODS

a sculpture by Thomas Crawford

Crawford's piece declares at once its distance
from the heartlessness of the sculpture's matrix:
a broadside ballad telling of an uncle's orders
that his niece and nephew—nuisances to him
in one version, rivals for a legacy in another—
be put to death.
The only softness permitted by the tale:
brother and sister are not murdered, merely
abandoned to die on their own in the woods.

Not ravaged by hunger, nor attacked
by animals, nor in a state of decay,
Crawford's siblings lie untouched,
cozily wrapped together, in a marmoreal nap
surely prelude to entrance into heaven.
Poised beside the boy, a bird stands, ready
to bury the two with what the woods offer.
It has yet to lay a leaf on them—nothing
mars their palpable perfection.

Intent on instances of life at its most intense,
Keats's urn did not picture death,
while Crawford's sculpture abandons itself
to lives ended, but only in a way that declares
with St. Paul: "Oh Death, where is thy sting?"

THE BLUES: A VARIATION

It's sky's heavenly blues,
like those going dark
this frigid winter afternoon,
that make one reluctant
to leave the earth, hung out
though it may be to dry.
No matter that they're nothing
but illusion, a supreme veiling
of the star-studded blackness
always just behind them—
they give a flawless performance,
making their regular disappearances
seem like measured withdrawals
into the wings, not the unmaskings
of the ultimate in backdrops.
There's no business like show business.

SPHERE

A Latino kid is passing my porch
on his bicycle. He's not pedaling,
he doesn't need to, the street's slight incline
a guarantee the bike will keep moving.
The bike is silent. He is motionless.

He's too young to see it that way,
but he's inside a bubble of perfection,
his stillness joined to the bike's motion,
the world flowing by him all on its own.

I have been there, though not recognizing it
any more than he does now. Only
its long-ago disappearance
enables us to perceive so sweet a sphere.

CUTE

What a gift—the sight, this morning,
of a family of foxes, not fifty yards
from the family-room window.
Two kits cavorted, as if
life were nothing but a big play pen.
We could not stop looking at them,
bringing them closer with the binoculars,
stripped of their reputation for, well, foxiness,
and proof against any thoughts of
chickens or cats suddenly clutched by the throat.
The kits were one thing, and one thing only—cute.
The invoking of that category, especially as it reaches
across species, is surely peculiarly human
What chipmunks, woodchucks, or raccoons
ever look at our young, even our Shirley Temples,
and think the equivalent of "Awww, how cute" ?
Thinking that, no, feeling that, makes for a precious
compound, one part aesthetic, one part love.

Would we could all have many such moments,
to help balance our revulsions, disdainings,
our looking through binoculars the wrong way
at the ugly, the tasteless, the cruel, the bizarre.
After all, the human embodiments of these
were probably all, at one time, cute.

INSTANT KING

Seed-obsessed, turbulent life
at the tree feeder, ceaseless
flurry of birds and squirrels

spun suddenly away by a blur
of air becoming a Cooper's Hawk
settling his outsize presence

on the biggest branch, slow-
folding his wings, showing his white breast,
instant king of an emptied realm

he views with disdain—tarrying but
a moment he takes his imperial business
elsewhere, leaving nothing behind

but an edict: brief as it was, record this reign.

ICE DANCERS

What have they to do with us,
perfect bodies in perfect union
moving through a fusion
of sweeps, glides, swirls, lifts,
fashioning a continuum of the improbable poised
always on the edge of disaster—
how long can gravity and error
be kept at bay?—
they're as lightly in touch with the ice
as a jet with the tarmac
the instant before takeoff,
their relation to our locomotion
as miniscule as the width of their blades.

KATZKOPF

(Katzkopf: Yiddish term, literally "cathead,"
used to designate somebody as stupid)

for Kassie

Restless, restless, she appears, and
disappears, unable to settle for life
that is merely cozy and pampered.
She needs it to be, at the very least,
interesting, better yet, a game, still
better, a game spiced with a pinch
of danger, something to merit
the intensity of her staring eyes.

Rutted in the daily round of things,
I find her hunger unreasonable,
draining. Why can't she agree
to live within life's limits? I do. But then
again, give her credit for refusing,
in that little Katzkopf of hers,
to submit to the ooze of the ordinary,
for insisting that life sizzle and spark
on its way to the hollow at the core of things.

MUCH ADO

Thanks to Kassie's self-imposed
24/7 bug patrol, a small black
thing has been spotted this windy
March night on the upstairs floor,
and instantly classified by me,
ignorant of all things insectine,
as belonging to Coleptera incognita.
Right now it's not moving. If still
alive, it will be dabbed to death
by Kassie, a cat even if an angel.
And what is the silly bugger
doing here to begin with,
appearing at a time still winter-
pinched, and in a space without
bug food, whatever that might be?
The thing starts to crawl.

My wife, spooked by insects, but
tender-hearted to a fault, cries out
it must be saved, and who but me
for the job, knight in shining pajamas?
I try to get it onto a piece of paper,
but displaying a stubbornness out of all proportion
to its size, it steadily refuses to mount
what could be its magic carpet, turning,

in slow motion, this way and that, this
way and that. Finally, it yields. Triumphant,
I lift up the paper with its tiny black burden,
and descend to the cellar. In transit, it crawls,
from top side to bottom, bottom to top.
Unlike me, it can't possibly know what's
going on, and also unlike me, it's blowing off
gravity. I set it on the floor, leaving it
to the mystery of its little life.

UNLOOKED-FOR VISITOR

Propelled by the mysterious
scheme of things, a sudden squatter,
abrupt bug, its pure blackness plopped
on a white sheet, frozen, is facing my computer.
Does it, too, want to go online, join
the contemporary after descending
from the prehistoric? Just how far back
can it trace its ancestry? Here, it seems
settled into intense contentment.

How can something this small, silent,
unmoving, so distract me from
the screen, so command my attention?
I finally break its spell, carefully carry it
on its sheet downstairs, consign it to the night,
whose blackness it exceeds.

TRANSLATIONS

I've taken to running an Insect Relocation Service,
though I'm my only customer and don't particularly
want your business. The bugs in question are mainly ants,
both red and black, the first small and bumbling,
the second comparatively Brobdignagian, though hardly
        ponderous,
capable of swift shifts into a mode best described as manic.

The weather has turned warm, and in Ant-ese this apparently
gets translated as: "Time to range freely over Alan's kitchen
        counters,
where one is sure to pick up a morsel or two, because try
as he might, he never gets rid of all of the crumbs. Also,
check out the cats' dishes, only rarely licked clean
by those creatures, who are capable of leaving over
great quantities of the gourmet contents."

I could simply smash the buggers or swipe them
with the sponge, treating them as crawling crumbs,
but loss and old age have turned me tender
toward almost all forms of life, and the ants, after all,
aren't much different from you and me when we wander
down a strange avenue, looking for a bite to eat,
hardly a reason for being instantaneously translated
into the next world.

Thus, picking them up with a wet tissue,
applying just enough pressure to prevent them
from making a run for it up my arm, but not so much
as to crush them, I translate them
to the rear deck where with a toss,
I abandon them to the rest of their lives, which,
we must remember, have been made possible
by many of the same Big Bang mind-boggling
ramifications that brought us here—
you, me, the ants, willy-nilly companions
in this slim quantum of space-time.

THE CAT SEEKS THE LIGHT

At the shelter where I found him, or,
rather, he found me, leaping into my lap
as I momentarily rested on a ratty sofa,
they told me, that in addition to his having been
the one to catch a mouse so foolish
as to have wandered into that place,
he had a fondness for chasing the little red dot
projected on the wall by a toy laser.

Having been adopted and brought home,
having emerged from his 24-hour disappearance
into the nearest closet, having boldly broken out
of the room he'd been confined in so as to avoid
his being overwhelmed by his new surroundings,
he has in fact proved to be a devotee of that laser,
but even more, of any moving light cast where he happens
to spot it, the sunbeam being flipped off the white surface
of the opening or closing refrigerator door,
the random reflections bouncing off my watch crystal,
the brilliant sliding circle I deliberately produce for him
by snaring the sun in my shaving mirror.

Still, he has proved more than a light-chaser—
he is also a light-contemplative (if you allow for
a slowly swishing tail), watching, watching,
before he makes his mad, futile dashes
trying to nail the elusive, skimming brightness.

Why should he not be so obsessed? He is himself
light, light furred, light pawed, light plume-tailed,
light whiskered, light yellow-eyed, scion of the sun,
the baby son I never had, no longer bearing
his shelter name of "Tommy," but the only name
I could have given him, given his incomparable
sweetness, my Honey Boy.

WHAT WERE YOU?

Honey Boy has taken to slipping
into the garage at every turn,
secreting himself there for hours.
What's with that cat? Is it possible
he had been an auto mechanic
in a former life? Is that any less
plausible than Joan Shmo having been
an Egyptian princess? How is it
that no one in a past life ever
emptied the chamber pots at Versailles?

MICK JAGGER, EAT YOUR HEART OUT

When I'm lying in bed with the door open,
Honey Boy inevitably enters and jumps
aboard, plopping himself right up against me,
so that we are spooning.

Few things have ever given me such satisfaction
as the feel of his deep, orange fur, and no one else,
neither spouse nor lover, has ever purred
simply for being stretched by my side.

WONDROUS HEART

You gotta have it.
You can not have it.
It can ache.
It can break.
It's subject to arrest.
It can be hard.
It can be soft.
You can speak from it.
It can be made of gold.
It can be made of stone.
It can be donated.
It can be transplanted.
It can be pierced
It can race.
It can pound.
You can find it in your mouth.
It's mocked if it bleeds.
You can set it on something.
You can wear it on your sleeve.
You can lose it.
If sacred, it can be a church.
It has a bottom.
You can eat it out.
You can cross it.
It can be attacked.
It can close the valves of its attention.
It can fail.
You can leave it in San Francisco.

WILD HORSES

It's an afternoon in June, about 2 P.M.,
sunny, breezy, dry, a perfect day
for staining the rear deck.
The chimes are doing their clinking best
but they don't stand a chance against
Mick Jagger on the portable radio
I've brought out, wailing his way through
"Wild Horses." No swagger in this number,
just straight lament with a touch of the tender.

The blue of the sky is in my eyes,
the smell of the stain in my nostrils,
the sounds of the Stones in my ears.
I don't ever want to die.
Wild horses couldn't drag me away.

ONE LOOKS AT ONE

I feel at home in the woods.
Trees, upright and fallen,
the uneven ground's soil
and leafy miscellany, the aroma
of earth, always fit me comfortably.

But today, on a walk, I suddenly
find myself nearly face to face
with a doe. She bounds away,
though for just a few feet, turns,
and stares at me. I stare back,

And I think that for all the ease
woods' flora brings me, their fauna
are something else, startling,
and because of that, carrying,
if only for a second, the flavor
of danger, followed by the wish
to connect in some undefined way
that never arrives.

THE CROSSING

After a breakfast of cereal, coffee, and bickering,
we were speeding to make the train,
when, swiftly magnifying in the windshield,
a slender young mother appeared
together with her three fairy-tale fawns.

Panicked by our rushing approach,
she churned in slow motion in mid-highway,
then, as we screeched to a halt,
finally made her crossing,
followed by those three picture-book tagalongs.

Why had she chosen so dangerous a route,
that beautiful dumb blonde,
more moving than any damsel in distress?
You saw her as dazed by her maternity,
the victim of a hit-and-run buck.
I only know that, fearful, fragile,
she changed the morning,
an almost helpless goddess.

ON THE ESTATE FARM

Walking a trail, I see random clusters of them,
the few calves either grazing like veterans,
or else determinedly attached to their mothers'
teats, the adults in tree-shade, motionless, silent,
so much bulk with so little will to impose,
a beautiful lack of intention in their big black eyes,
a perfect fit of bovine bodies and being-ness.

A noise in the distance draws my attention —
at the far end of a field, I see
a single file of cows moving at a steady pace,
not trotting, and nobody in sight
either leading or goading them,
yet seemingly caught up in a forced march —
they are sending forth a cacophony of moos,
bellows, blaws, sounds beyond our vocabulary,
cries of creatures at the mercy of some human purpose —
are they all being led to slaughter, to serve
the estate's celebrated four-star restaurant?

Should you know, please keep it to yourself.

NEVER MIND

On seeing Dina Michener's photograph "Head"

Snout stunningly sticking straight up, eyes closed,
in massive, well-earned repose, the great bovine head
dominates the frame.
Never mind that the body is elsewhere.
Never mind that the innocent-looking liquid
you see is not water but blood. Never mind
the panic, the stunning, the skinning, the hacking,
that have taken place off-camera.
Never mind how animals were sacrificed to the gods.
Never mind how they are sacrificed to us.
Never mind how fear and appetite justify anything.
If you value your sleep, never mind.

ON SEEING A CARTOON BY HARRY BLISS
IN THE NEW YORKER

Skull propped on something indeterminate (a rock?),
a coffined skeleton imagines skeleton sheep jumping over a rail
      fence,
one at a time, the whole thing taking place underground in a bony
      parody
of something that has probably never helped any living soul to fall
      asleep.

Witty as hell, but for me, a major claustrophobe, it evokes
my worst nightmare—retaining consciousness after death,
not in some spirit form floating free, but locked forever
in quarters tighter than those imposed by torturers,
tighter than the car trunks TV bad guys are always putting
live people into, and with the possibility, as in the scene at hand,
of insomnia, the cartoon denying what many of us have counted
        on
as a sure thing—death as eternal sleep.

Not funny—witty is not necessarily funny,
Harry Bliss, you with your dubious surname,
you channeling Charles Addams.
How about I rename you?
How about Harry Sadist?

THE END

When, after the crawl's credits
have finally come to the elongated,
egg-shaped icon, and you know that
it's really the end, you have no excuse
for continuing to sit there in that stunned
state movies can induce; you have been
taken in and now you are being cast out
into the lobby and the street, still carrying
your sorrow or exhilaration but not knowing
what to do with either, cinema once again
having hatched its long-running plot
to render real life second-best.

STATES OF TRUCE

Whether by human hands or by chance,
these massive stones sit side by side
at the foot of the hill, holding back
the earth from sliding down and obliterating
the measured town walk—soil and stones
in an ongoing truce of taut tonnage.

How many other standstills we depend on,
as with our planet's speed being great enough
to hold us in place against the sun's attempt
to suck us back into its fierce furnace, but not
so great as to break free of the sun's lasso
holding our home from flying into endless space.
Then there's the virtual agreement of land and sea
to maintain their restless boundary (suspended,
I grant, for the occasional tsunami, and now threatened
by oceans rising)—or the balanced
exchange of oxygen and carbon dioxide
between plants and animals, making possible
the myriad species of each continuing.
These large arrangements have kept everything going.

Not so at the level of our cells, nothing there
to counter the ruthless snipping away
of their protective telomeres, no means
of replenishment, our bodies trapped in a losing war,
a nano-truce simply outside the scheme of things.

THE DEFIANT ONES

Whether in repose in their houses,
or—screaming bullies—hurling
themselves down the street,
fire engines are inevitably beautiful,
looking as if they had just been
unwrapped, their brass and red metal
making for a Platonic form on earth.

Unignorable, their sirens announce
their glossy defiance of what may lie
before them—flame's hideous appetite,
bodies hurling themselves into space,
charred wood, charred children,
suffocating smoke and its aftermath,
the persistent stench of the burnt.

Shine on, fire engines, screech and gleam,
as, night or day, you cast your light
into the darkest of places.

GOING COCKEYED TO THE (OLD) WHITNEY

I'm glad to be in the street, escaped at last
from the retina specialists' town house.
I'd waited two hours, then gotten an exam
with an instrument descended from medieval torturers.
I'm still cockeyed from the damned dilating drops,
but, feeling I've earned some pleasure, decide
to go to the Whitney, where my eyes will be able
to make out something. Not so fast.
About to plunk my money down, I mention
the particular show I've mainly come for.
Sorry, it ended three days ago. Great.
Going into my reflex sulk I stalk out,
throwing myself on the city itself as performance artist.
I suppose you can say it comes through.

I am accosted twice by beggars, one of them
asking if I have a twenty to spare.
I know this is the Upper East Side but still....
A petite street lady goes briskly from garbage pail
to garbage pail, seeking something she can't seem to find.
Two separate guys are talking to themselves.
No, they're not using hands-free cell phones,
they're talking to themselves in the good, old-fashioned,
crazy New York way, one doing your basic mumble,
the other shouting angrily that they'll get away
with it, they always do, look at O.J.
Countless women, some coatless, even
on this chilly day, stand in front of doorways,
taking drags as if their lives depended on it.

Over on Lexington, a fire-engine siren is doing its best
to fry everyone's hearing. The God who parted
the Red Sea could make Himself useful here.
But for now the engine has to crawl its way
through the traffic, just like everybody else.

I finally board the bus to Grand Central, where my train will take me away from all this, the city's insane bounty, and hand me over to the inane bareness of the burbs.

ULTIMATE BLING

I have gotten a freebee with my delivery
from Haband (a cheapo mail-order house).
It's a watch (made by some anonymous

firm), which, together with its stainless steel
band, possesses a glitter so intense
it could launch a hip hop career.

Beside the knurled stem, the watch boasts
two knobs, their functions mysterious,
since the thing has come without instructions.

The face has three auxiliary circles, aspiring suns,
the light coming off them making it
impossible for you to see what the hour is.

The whole thing is useless, one of the best gifts
I've ever received. At last, wearing it,
I shall be liberated from time.

TIME IS NOT ON MY SIDE

The river glideth at his own sweet will...
—Wordsworth

Just emerged from the shower,
after having failed to keep an eye
on the time, I realize I have but
fourteen minutes to towel off,
get dressed and get down
to the train, a walk that normally
takes me about five minutes.

By virtue of not tying my shoelaces,
nor buckling my belt properly,
nor buttoning my shirt, nor combing
my hair, nor strapping on my watch,
(simply tossing it into a pocket),
I arrive at the station just in time,
a frantic collection of loose ends.

Taking my seat on the train has never
been more welcome, and, as always,
I gaze at the Hudson, unruffled,
sweetly taking its time, barely
showing which way it is flowing
beneath the rippling surface.
I could, if I wanted to, get off
at Spuyten Duyvil or Riverdale,
and fling my watch, this tiny,
ticking tyrant, into the river,
letting that long-time symbol

of Time effortlessly swallow
one of its puny representatives,
my act a stand-in for throwing
myself into the wide waters,
swimming not a stroke, but floating
on my back, alternately contemplating the sky
and closing my eyes, barely
conscious of moving, letting the river
have its way with me, taking me
away from the frenzied, the frenetic,
for good.

HUCK, JIM, AND YOU

You could just kvetch at this sudden
crawling of the commuter train
in its approach to the Tarrytown station,
or you could look out the window
and watch the necklace of lights
on the Tappan Zee Bridge gradually
coming into view, a private showing
for you or anyone ceasing to journey
on a charging train, lying back instead
on the raft it has decided to become.

VIEW FROM THE HUDSON LINE

Riding backwards in a railroad car, everything
recedes as soon as it comes into view,
a series of ruthless removals, try as our eyes might
to hang on to any given sight. But riding backwards
into the future, as each of us does, unable to know
what lies ahead, things we'd like not to see
persist in appearing, pains we have given,
pains received, words we cannot believe we uttered,
words we cannot believe we didn't, a landscape
conjured up by memory's ruthless recall.

ROMA

sprezzatura (It.): an air of nonchalance,
conveying effortlessness

Every now and then, from a distance,
you'll spot what you'd swear is a bunch
of rags dumped on the sidewalk, but which,
on closer approach, proves to be
the motley covering of a human form
set in a motionless, shrunken (fetal?) posture,
the only indicator of the person beneath
a small portion of exposed arm stretched forth,
its hand holding a cup. Hard to imagine
anything more abject, begging brought
to a mute, faceless apotheosis. Just beyond
the cup, motorcycles roar by, brilliantly
piloted by hydrocephalic-helmeted
drivers, all verve and nerve, cocky
gladiators threading through the traffic,
their sprezzatura lost on the beggars,
who seem to have lost everything.

LAMENT

Pens are failing all over America,
in banks, post offices, gas stations,
at supermarket check-out counters,
unable to produce even enough ink
to eke out one's measly signature,
making necessary irritable pressings
and scratchings with just spotty results.

Where are the pens of yesteryear?
Ay, where are they?

I mean way yesteryear,
those "fountain" jobs (just consider
the name), that having thirstily drawn in
bottled ink gave it back in flowing
abundance, and so generously as
to stain blue the insides of our middle fingers'
upper joints, subdued to what they worked with.

Ball points? Roller balls?
Just hold up their itty-bitty business ends
to the light, and compare them to the elegant
concave curvings of the fountains' prominent steeples.

I'm pretty close to writing off this age.

SHOWTIME AT SUNSET

The earth turns and suddenly it's showtime
again, the day's rheostat having slid
into place another spectacular ending,
our world, sideswiped by light,
cast as a luminous version of itself,
each part, without the slightest expenditure
of effort, compelling our gaze,
the ordinary—trees, houses, cars—
serving as featured players, every last thing
lit to a brilliant wattage by our sinking star,
every last thing in new, shining vestments,
a final gift to those on the edge of the dark.

THE PRIESTLY BLESSING

kohanim: (Hebrew) priests

Gathered at the front of the synagogue,
facing us, their heads and extended arms
covered by fringed prayer shawls,
hands held together in a prescribed shape,
the priests intone their blessing,
repeating—one word at a time—
what the cantor first sings out.

The congregants' eyes are turned
away, obediently avoiding exposure
to such splinters of God's light
as might be emanating from His vessels.

Just prior to uttering the final word,
the kohanim deliver a lulling,
wordless melody, then shift
abruptly to a kind of shout,
"Shalom" almost hurled at us, its syllables
breaking over our heads, a blessing,
to my young ears, being delivered
with the force of a curse.

AN EIGHTH DAY

Porcupined by the acupuncturist,
I lie here, puzzled as to why some needles
are making me ache, while others are not,
the larger question being: why must
there be pain at all? Couldn't we have
so evolved as to have been immune to it,
our nerves so formed as to register only pleasure?
Or was it that God said (as recorded in some
yet to be discovered parchment), "Let there
be pain," and there was pain, and God saw
that it was good (remember His mysterious ways).

Could I but say "Let there be no sciatica,"
and there was no sciatica, and I saw that it
was good, and there was evening and there
was morning, an eighth day, and I rested.

TO ONE WHO TOLD ME I WAS NOT MAKING ADEQUATE USE OF MY TIME AND SHOULD GET A JOB

Descending from the peak of Mount Everest into Tibet,
I arranged with the Chinese for the release of ten monks
and for their being transported to the residence of the Dalai
        Lama
in India. I then met with representatives of that country
and Pakistan, and presided over an agreement reducing
their nuclear arsenals and granting Kshmir independence..
Putting in a call to George Soros, I got him to pledge
25 million dollars for an incentives fund aimed at inducing
American fat kids to lose at least 20 pounds each. After a short
        nap,
I jetted to Gaza, meeting with liberals and right-wingers
from Israel along with representatives of al-Fatah,
Hamas and Hezbollah, managing by sheer force of personality
to help forge a two-state, lands-for-peace arrangement between
the Israelis and Palestinians. Tomorrow I will do
forty push-ups and turn my attention to the problem
of health care in America. After that, Afghanistan.
Today, I wrote this poem.

CURTAILED

The satisfying snipping sound of the clipper
as I trim my nails, steel curtailing keratin,
its persistent impulse to sneakily extend
itself, thought to continue after we die,
though Google tells us that is not the case,
it's more a matter of the skin around
the nails retracting due to the cutting-off
of the glucose that has fed them.

Whoever thought the thought of death
would put an end to the thought of pleasure
this poem started with? I guess it's one
more triumph of the grave, curtailing
the possibility of the sonnet I thought I'd write.

SNOWSTORM

White, white, white has been this day,
countless, weightless crystals
coalescing to a bough-breaking heaviness,
their silent descent muffling day's usual noises,
though scraping snowplows soon try
to assert themselves, resist the mass
burial the storm seems intent upon.

Who can like the expense and effort
that will be required to dig out from under
this semi-wet blanket? But who can
deny the pleasure of seeing our world,
if only temporarily, stripped
of our routines and intentions,
converted into a glowing tabula rasa?

CROW IN JANUARY

What is it about this falling
snow that has provoked that
crow to keep cawing its guts out?

Is it a matter of pure blackness
being offended by pure whiteness
tyrannically imposing itself on all,
however light its footprint?

Or is this insistent bird a reincarnation
of Melville's Ishmael, for whom whiteness
"shadows forth the heartless voids
and immensities of the universe"?

Crow, you are but a black dot
on a great albino landscape,
but keep up your possibly important
work, caw on, raucous one, caw on.

FREEING UP THE BUSHES

Thanksgiving 2002

If for nothing else we should give thanks
at the sight of this early, clinging snowfall,
which, after the dervish dance of flakes,
has come to dress each bush and branch
in the whitest of cotton, as if made ready
for First Communion.

So much for first impressions.
For, considering further, you can see
the holly, boxwood, and rhododendron
(to say nothing of our only evergreen's lower branches),
bent to the ground under the seeming weightlessness
of this virginal visitation, this silent epiphany.

The snow's brute beauty—this is a touch
of Melville's whiteness, of Frost's.

I take a broom, go outside,
and gingerly apply upward pats to each bush,
freeing it to assume its original greenness.
Each eventually springs upright, intact,
with the exception of the left-most rhododendron.
A chunk of it has snapped off
and I must now regard this long, thick stem, leaf-laden,
grown so slowly but surely over five years,
as so much junk, to be tossed
onto the graveyard of brown leaves bordering the lawn.
Whiteness has claimed another sacrifice.

MARCH TALKS BACK

"March, you blowhard bitch of a month,
flinging snow-flurries in our faces,
playing hide and seek with warmer days,
mocking the clothes we thought
would be adequate, turning dirt roads
into mud-fests, who needs you?

What's that you're saying?"

"True, I favor winter, and am close
to Aeolus, who lets me borrow
his invisible, unruly minions
at a moment's notice, converting
my hosting of Spring's start
into a farce; yet despite all that,
I am to be pitied, not detested,
for April *is* the cruelest month,
utterly refusing to extend my lease—
Time's winds are blowing us all away."

SPRING PUZZLES

I

Pink confetti lines curbs, is scattered
on sidewalks, but left over from what parade?
Surely we would have heard the music.
Oh, now I get it. This wonderful stuff
descended in silence, tossed into the air
by crab-apple trees, impatient with
mere beauty, eager to settle into nondescript
green and grow their mouth-puckering fruit—
it is not only we who are perverse.

II

Snow is falling on our tennis match,
not flakes, but bits of fluff,
scattering or gathering in pools,
some of it hitching rides on the balls,
fuzz irresistibly drawn to fuzz,
getting whacked for its temerity,
the whole scene wonderful, absurd,
not one iota of fluff able to take
root on the hard surface—
but what do the cottonwood trees know,
except that it's time for their letting go.?

DOWNED

Unreal, as the unexpected often seems,
a young buck is lying on the dividing line
of the Saw Mill Parkway northbound,
not visibly injured but undeniably downed,
not even trying to get up. Traffic has been
slowed to a crawl, and as I inch by the buck
I think how beautiful, how helpless,
the two thoughts coeval, the buck emblematic
of all lovely flesh at odds with circumstance.
I am on the edge of tears.

Looking in the rear-view mirror
as I drive slowly away, I see
traffic has stopped completely,
while a young woman is determinedly
making her way toward the buck,
and I think of course, that's what
I should have done.

In all probability she will not
be writing a poem about the matter,
that's not what doers do,
that's for helpless, sensitive spectators,
downed by lack of imagination.

IN THE BASEMENT

I'm beginning what I've managed to avoid
for so long, an archaeological dig
in the basement, starting to go
through cartons still unpacked
in the more than seven years
we've been living in this house that we built.
True, we brought the place into the world
with more than
the classic difficulty—
who could have faced these cartons
after those birth pangs? Later,
we just avoided the damned things.
More scary than a madwoman in the attic
is a ton of unopened stuff in the basement.
Even now I think I should just haul
everything, sight unseen,
to the town dump. I mean,
what worthwhile shards of our earlier life
could possibly turn up? We've gotten
along without any of them all this time.
But lacking the courage to simply
trash the past, unable, being human,
to live in a pure present
like our cat Kassie—she's prowling around
down here, enjoying the general mess,
it's just one more adventure for her—
I begin the work of excavation.

Okay, what's in this box that resists
my ripping it open? Looks like a grab bag—
must have been packed in a last desperate
effort to get everything out of the old house
before the onslaught of the movers—
a blue plastic shoe horn, a spool
of black thread, a heart-shaped glass dish,
some cheap jewelry, a combination lock—
flotsam and jetsam, a modern midden.

But wait, some of the miscellany tales a shape—
a parochial school graduation pin,
a high school honor society medal,
a Phi Beta Kappa key, a Ph.D. diploma—
there they are, emblems of my climb
up the ladder of academe. But where are they?
Just more stuff, upscale detritus.
Maybe, as Wordsworth said, we come here
trailing clouds of glory, but for certain we leave
trailing clusters of junk.
That's why we need garbage men
more than CEOs.

I'm about to toss the box when I realize
it's got one more thing—looks like a really old
photograph folder. Jesus!
It contains my parents' wedding picture.
I don't recall ever seeing it, my mother
in a gorgeous gown and headpiece,
looking solemn, almost terrified
(late in her life she told me she hadn't loved
the groom, had married him on the rebound).
And my father—was he ever really that young?
I'm probably twice the age he was in the picture.
How can that be? Photographs are two-faced,
dramatizing the passage of time, even while
dissolving it. His youth apart, who is this dude,
looking coolly at the camera? He could
pass for an aspiring Mafioso or be an understudy
for George Raft. So where did he go when I
showed up? I think I'll leave the other boxes unopened.
For the present at least, I've had enough of the past.

"IN THE PORCHES OF MY EARS"

Not likely to make most people's top-ten lists
of their favorite Shakespearean passages,
but it's always knocked me out, that place in Hamlet
where the Ghost tells of how he was poisoned
by his brother's pouring the "juice of cursed hebenon…
in the porches of my ears," the poison coursing
through him, covering his "smooth body" with
a leper-like "vile and loathsome crust…."
A touch of narcissism, perhaps, in that
"smooth body," but still, you get the point.

I think of the Ghost as I lie here this morning,
relieved to have escaped the murk and anxious strainings
of my dreams, but, with the radio tuned to NPR,
news of the bad dream of the world is being poured
into my ears, a brew of bombs, lies, stupidity and greed,
turning the brief respite of my waking into
a consciousness crusted with rage and despair.
The Ghost was done in by Claudius, but I have only myself
to blame for this recurrent tuning
in, this violation by ear. It's as if
I say "Give us this day our daily poisoning,"
clicking on the radio, granting myself the dose.

IVORY

I should shut it off, but I don't,
this Leonard Lopate interview
with the author of an article
on the world-wide trade in ivory,
an enterprise herding elephants
toward extinction. My rage is rising,
along with a sense of helplessness,
and then a fantasy of omnipotence
in which I accost the poachers, render them
impotent, and pull out all their teeth, saying
"See, here is your very own ivory—
sell this to the Chinese for their chopsticks."

But all that has happened of course
is my having taken in one more dose
of the depression-food the radio
dispenses so abundantly, each day,
each day, each day.

NOT BEYOND PETROLEUM

Piercing, the persistent sight
of that angry boiling, furiously
frothing, thick, brownish gunk,
thrusting upward, a wound
pouring forth its petroleum pus
into the life-laden Gulf waters.

What audit will ever tally the true cost
of our imperious drills, our beloved cars,
those servants turned masters?

The world seems poised over a gulf.
Have we emerged from the mothering oceans
only to become a race of matricides?

SUNDAY, JUNE 21, 2009, 7 P.M.

Even this, longest of days, must come to an end.
It is not so much a matter of darkness descending,
as of the landscape's being slowly enveloped
in a deep green sadness, inescapable.
There must be something about Sunday evenings
doing its work here, just as it did when, a boy
of the city streets, I found myself in its soft
grip, dosed with a mysterious melancholy,
far worse than the cod liver oil
my mother obliged me to take each morning.
That could be gotten past quickly, displaced
by juice, milk and cereal, but the Sunday-
evening blues were beyond any quick fix,
and, here now, don't seem to have changed
even as sumer is icumen in.

SUMMER SOLSTICE + ONE, 2013

Just about to enter my cottage,
I looked up to see a moon that appeared bigger
than any moon has a right to be,
a lunar heavyweight that, especially brilliant,
still allowed one to look at her,
as the sun at full blast never does,
the sun that must be clothed in clouds
to make its descents beautiful,
while the full, nude moon, rising, requires
only itself to attract our gaze, draw forth
the wanton worship of our eyes.

SURPRISE!

Perverse hydrangea, you've been holding out
on me. Judging from your appearance
each time I walk up the gravel path to the house,
you have decided to go wholly green this year
(your contribution to the environment?),
nary a blossom in sight, as opposed
to the rhodies and azaleas crowded up
against you, which have done their usual
flowery duty without a murmur,
pouring forth their colors in profusion.
Anal-Retentive, you disappoint me.

On a whim, I walk to the far end of the porch,
the better to take a closer look at you,
though you hardly deserve it.
Surprise! Your back parts, well hidden
up till now, are happily burdened
with blooms, explosions of pink lobes,
a floral fireworks display, unfading,
held in suspension, large reward
for the small trouble I have taken
to get close to you.

Whatever I thought of you up till now,
I see that it is simply a matter of your having,
for some reason, turned shy this year.
Don't worry—I shall not give
away your secret, except of course, here.

SUN-STRUCK

Not quite round, therefore not quite
perfect, but still damned beautiful,
this orange disc, posted in the heavens,
has laid upon the river waters
an orange stripe, which, weightless,
floats shimmeringly.

But is that true, the weightlessness
I mean—or does the sun's photon
progeny have a measurable mass?
I leave that to the physicists, but know
that sunlight on an aged face, basking
in its warmth, strikes with merciless weight.

SUNSET IN LUCI'S GARDEN

Was any failure ever as beautiful
as the slow-motion fading of this light,
accompanied by the steady,
undaunted gurgling of the fountain,
sight and sound benignly conspiring
to enfold us in this Catskills cocoon?
Praise the movement of water,
praise, praise the dying of the light.

SEPTEMBER 11, 2009

Things fall apart; the centre cannot hold;
—W.B. Yeats

Yeats was wrong—things don't fall apart;
they don't hang together to begin with.
Melville knew this, in his description
of the usual, beheaded whale carcass
cast off by the captor ship: "still colossal,"
torn at by acres of sharks and screaming fowl,
a "hideous sight," set beneath "the unclouded
and mild azure sky, upon the fair face
of the pleasant sea, wafted by the joyous breezes…"

9/11 should have been like today,
chilly, gray, rainy—instead it was gorgeous,
September taking a page out of early October,
brilliant backdrop to the two poisoned arrows
targeted on the helpless fat towers,
to the piercing, the fires, the collapse,
the most monumental of presences turned
to toxic rubble, choking air, vanished bodies,
all of it under that clear blue sky no longer
viewable from the ground, but still visible,
if you got high enough or far away enough,
to where the gods are, such gods as may be.

CHURCH OF 9/11

St. Paul's, at Broadway and Vesey,
you who have long declared yourself
the oldest public building in continuous
use in America, I hereby re-christen you,
acknowledge your self-transformation.

Relieved only by the gated graveyard's
lush grass and flowered borders,
your gray bricks and drab brown columns
are hardly inviting. Still, you proved
sanctuary in the days following
New York's worst wounding,
ministering to rescue workers and residents,
acquiring a landmark status well
beyond the boast of your longevity,
beyond the pew once occupied
by George Washington, a status
grounded on a monumental
disappearance.

Your chapel has replaced itself.
No pews now, only chairs, many turned
away from your altar, and towards
a banner bringing greetings from Oklahoma
to New York and the rescue workers.
On this day, that altar has drawn
but a single worshiper, kneeling at its rail.
All others here are tourists, many with cameras,
slowly circulating among a series
of folk shrines memorializing the disaster.

One features photos of rescue workers,
another heaps together cloth emblems
from scores of police departments,
yet another positions countless strings
of origami above a veritable army
of teddy bears—what to make
of this juxtaposition?
Perhaps we can't go beyond
what the plaque accompanying

the small back-wall quilt says,
that chaos reigned everywhere,
that the quilt is unfinished,
"the batting...exposed and charred...
the threads...not trimmed—reflecting
the vast number of lives that were so
unfinished when the World Trade Center
was destroyed..."

So there is no comfort from above
to be found in this place, only
the companionship of shared sorrowing,
only the celebration of selfless rescuers
(however little they were able to rescue),
only the making of small artifacts to defy
the sudden smoke-filled absence
where monoliths had reigned.

SERPENT

he shall bruise your head,
and you shall bruise his heel—
                              Genesis

The town's measured-mile walk
has a new marker today, a thick,
two-foot snake, lying right in the middle
of the path's end, dead, as confirmed
by my gingerly nudging its tail with my toe
(no question here of my bruising its head,
no question of its bruising my heel.)

The very tip of the tail is slightly flattened,
but the corpse is otherwise intact. What brought it
to this end? A close look reveals a skin
of subdued colors, subtly interwoven. Later Googling
suggests it might have been a banded water snake,
meaning it was not poisonous, but even if it were,
it had lost all its capacity to terrify, the muscular sinuousness
of its total being fallen to profound stillness,
having entered the realm opened up for us by its ultimate
        ancestor,
human and serpent companions now.

TENDING A GRAVESITE

for Elaine

Stupidly planted (who did it? who can remember?)
right up against our parents' tombstone,
yew, designed to soften the site, is now a dense bunch
of little dead branches and twigs, obscuring
"a woman of valor" and "a scholar, gentle and kind."

Why couldn't the gravestone have been left alone?
It has weathered the years well, offering
the endurance neither we nor the bush can.

Still, when I take out the garden shears
I have brought, and begin cutting away,
I must use great force to squeeze
the handles together, the brown yew
not only an unwanted momento mori,
but, in its remarkable resistance,
an illustration, perhaps, of a general law:
"Whatever is, wants to stick around."

LATE SUNDAY MORNING

Consider this newly-arrived fly,
crawling across my breakfast table,
and consider as well the multi-peaked,
barren, brown, bleak mountain filling
the restaurant's picture-window,
looking ready to surrender a portion
of itself to crush this establishment
along with its perfect lawn, nervily placed
at the mountain's foot, and see
if you can extrapolate what, exactly,
the Creator had in mind.

Alternatively, consider a neutrino
(any neutrino), and consider as well
a galaxy (any galaxy), and see if
you can attribute any mind at all
to the Creator, or only an irrepressible
urge to bring forth a wildly various, exploding
universe, embracing the infinitesimal
and the infinite, in a marriage
at once wondrous and ludicrous,
fiercely defying our grasp.

P.S.
Here are a series of teeny-tiny creeks
being squeezed out by a behemoth
of a mountain (not the one above),
another incongruity, but this one
making for a simple pleasure on my part,
suggesting that in musing on the nature of things,
one might just as well go with the flow.

LEDA AND THE SWAN, REVISITED

Zeus put fine feathers on
to do his fancy treading.
Now what crazy myth has hatched
to float and conquer through
the beauty of your throat?

UNCOUPLING

Like freight cars,
they come together,
man slamming into woman,
woman enclosing man.

Then something fails,
and each rolls solo
onto branch lines stretching
toward opposite horizons.

BURNT WORDS

Arrived home from work, I found
my living room converted
to a smoky stage, a one-woman drama
being enacted in silence, save for
the crackling in the background.

My wife of the time was tossing her collection
of my letters into the small fireplace,
already so filled with feathery ashes
it seemed they would spill out
beyond the raised hearth.

Over the phone, she had announced,
expending few words, she was leaving me,
and was now putting on this incineration
when she knew I would witness it.

Those letters had been my link to life,
much of my courtship, part of our implicit
engagement, while, a grad student, toiling far
from her, I pondered the words of others.

During that now quaint time, my letters had piled up,
as had hers, both sets lugged, after we'd married,
out to California and back.

Hers are still around, somewhere—
I haven't had the heart to burn them.
Eventually, I'll seek them out and toss
them into the trash, letting the town torch her words
for me, stirring them together with mine
in amorphous air, a realm of countless words
that might as well never have been.

SITTING FOR MY LIKENESS
WHILE DRIVING

Looking straight ahead,
you beside me,
I sit for my likeness
on the run.
Your words, rapid, precise,
present me to myself.
out of the corner of my eye.

You tell me I turn
a full profile
to each moment
as I race through the days,
intent only on the next chore.

You have struck
a perfect likeness
of your achiever,
emperor of speed,
not ice cream.

I grasp this new coin.
Ah, good, it burns my palm.

LATE MARRIAGE

Because we built it, the house
carried no history, and when you died,
only eight years after we moved in,
I was left to remember what had not
happened there—sudden hugs,
spontaneous bursts of fox-trotting
around the kitchen, half-comic,
half-sexy tangos in the basement,
silliness and teasings, discardings
of our respective grievances.

But at least, when the letter of acceptance
for your poems arrived, and you read
it aloud to me, we embraced,
and, in a wordless ceremony of shared tears,
pronounced ourselves man and wife.

NEAR SHARON GARDENS

Down comes the crossing gate, just
as I am about to drive over the tracks
and reach Presbrey-Leland Memorials,
to make final arrangements for your stone.

The commuter train clacks speeding by,
and suddenly I see each of its cars
as an elongated coffin, pressed
into temporary service by the living.

I don't need to know who's aboard,
all those flying past as you lie nearby.
I do know that each, sooner or later,
will leave his car for the last time,

enter into an exclusive compartment,
and never consult another schedule.

THIS DAY

You have been denied this day
along with all the other days since
the night you died, but it's this day,
this day, I would give you, could I
raise you from the dead, have you
enveloped in this Indian summer Sunday,
its soft clarity, its stillness, have you
stand in sunshine once more.

But all I can do is touch your footstone,
framed in its newness by bare dirt,
lit but not warmed by the sun.
I go down on my knees, press
my forehead to it, rise up
and, on the headstone we will share,
place a wildly assorted bouquet,
rather than the stone of Jewish custom

Driving home, I remember, too late,
how much you loved stones,
were always collecting them,
saying they had been called
supreme concentrations of energy.

Even after all these days,
I still don't get things right.

ON THE WAY TO THE HOSPITAL

Walking across the iron bridge at Marble Hill
vibrating with traffic, I spot a lone pigeon
on the ground, bobbing and pecking
as its kind does, but to what end I can't say.
The only thing resembling morsels
are salt grains, leftovers from the last
snow clean-up of this hard winter.

What is the creature doing here, all
by itself? Aren't city pigeons herd birds,
living out their lives in insistent clusters?
Has it broken some obscure pigeon law,
resulting in banishment to this bleak place?

Who can tell? But for the time being,
we share this bridge to the unknown.

SPUYTEN DUYVIL

In a midnight call, through tears,
you tell me your husband is leaving.

I am on my way to see you

Viewed through the train window, at Marble Hill,
the rapidly flowing Hudson is bearing
small islets of ice—they look like garbage.

At Spuyten Duyvil, the river, almost
entirely frozen over, seems struck
by a case of aquatic eczema, illuminated
by the half-hearted sunlight.

Why, in this world, with its infrastructure
of pain, do we do to each other what we do?

LOOKING WEST ON 42ND STREET AT TWILIGHT AFTER DAYS OF RAIN

Furrow of light effortlessly laid down
by the low-slung sun, pale green sky
above Grand Central, office towers
breaking out in spots of cool fluorescence,
oblivious crowds surging toward day's end,
no film or pixels to freeze any of it,
only this graphite scrawl on a scrap
of paper as my train pulls out.

CRUSOE IN TARRYTOWN

Walking into the darkening apartment, I see,
at the center of the kitchen island,
the scalloped, elaborately carved vase
mysteriously aglow, crystal suffused
with gold.

Of course—it's the sun casting level rays
through a back window, through the vase,
a gift of columnar, entangled light
briefly brightening my life,
my island.

INVASION BY THE BEETLES

No, that's not a misprint for Liverpool's
most distinguished alumni conquering us
half a century ago—and "invasion"
is admittedly a piece of hyperbole—
but I wanted to get your attention.

In short, I'm talking about bugs,
the ones, all of the same kind,
making mysterious midwinter
appearances in my cottage,
manifesting themselves, always solo,
wherever—on kitchen cabinet, counter,
bathroom sink, bedroom radiator cover,
the top of my head—
you name it.

Almost always, the creature is still—
heightening the effect of having simply
been secreted on the spot for some secret reason,
coming from nowhere, going nowhere—

On the rare occasion when it's moving,
so slow is the pace, it's as if it is crawling
through glue—what destination could it reach
in less than a lifetime?

I cannot help but ask about each what is on
its buggy, little mind—what does it want?
where does it think it's going?

Do we have here a small mystery or a large one?
Is there an ultimate scale by which my bugs
are judged inconsequential, as opposed
to us? Or are we being viewed by Something,
which finds people small, baffling, possibly pointless?

BIRD SURGE

At this distance, with my less
than perfect vision, the birds
floating on the sunset waters
of the reservoir appear to be
dabs of light, a few, faint, querulous
quacks seeming to come from some source
behind them. Suddenly, they rise,
and, accompanying their surge
with a communal cacophony,
fly off toward the disappearing sun.

What made them reject in an instant
their contented bobbing, and embrace
the effort of hauling themselves up into the air,
stretching vocal chords to the utmost?
Were they bored with their pastoral,
or frightened by something only
they could sense? Or did they realize,
in a flash, the sun was deserting them,
and resolve they would keep it in view
for as long as their strength held out?

NOT BAKED IN A PIE

As if flung upon the wind by some giant hand
seeding the air, a score or more of black birds,
wings furiously flapping in seeming panic and disorder
above Route 9, converts with shocking
swiftness into a still life: the birds, unmoving,
all perched on a wire above the speeding cars,
a magic trick pulled off by God knows what.

BECOMING BIRCH

As with any perfect day—this one lightly
touched by breezes—I want to enter
into something worthy of it, something
ebullient, adventurous.

But baffled as always as to what that might be,
I settle for sitting on the porch and gazing
at the four-trunked birch we planted
a decade ago, wishing I could become
a fifth, as still as the others, even as I indulge
the shimmer and glitter of my trembling leaves.

AT THE ZOO

Uncompanioned, the polar bear paces
back and forth on this October summer day,
head slightly raised, mouth steadily agape
as if it is seeking something from the air
other than mere oxygen, something
that might redeem its existence
on this steep, gray, rocky enclosure
a million miles from the blessedly frigid,
blessedly level, endless expanse
from which it has been plucked, white world
it will never be returned to, white world
slowly but surely going down to blue water,
the bear temporary cynosure of eyes
it will never meet, never acknowledge,
none of us worthy of its interest,
none of us able to heal it.

TENNYSON HAD IT ABOUT RIGHT

"Nature, red in tooth and claw..."
—from Tennyson's "In Memoriam"

If, as they say, history is written from the standpoint
of the victors, then the notion of Nature's beneficence
is surely derived from the perspective of carnivores,
whose neighborhoods have been thoughtfully stocked
with tasty grass-eaters, speedy of foot, but often
not speedy enough, as when an ibex, whose sole sin
is nibbling for a living, flees for its life down a Himalayan slope
only to be fatally seized by a pursuing snow leopard.
It does not matter that the leopard does not roar, yet
were there any justice at all, the ibex would be allowed
at least a shriek or two, so as to vent its panic, pain, despair,
but this is not opera, and its throat, not constructed
for such vocal display, and now strangled by fangs,
can produce only a few huffing sounds, the squeezing out
of its life muffled by the way it is outside the gates of Eden.

AURAL SEX

There would be no assignation—
you'd suddenly recalled another engagement,
one you couldn't break.
Next day, unexpected, longed for, a call
comes, bringing the dusky cello tone
your voice takes on only over the phone.
Even as you complain about fuzz on the brain,
you pour forth bon mots, comic cascades,
your wit twirling its tongue in the whorls of my ear.
I grow rigid with attention, eager not to miss a note,
then collapse into happiness. Absent, absent-minded siren,
did you know you were throwing me a lifeline?

SEX AND THE SEPTUAGENARIAN

Do bees fuck?

There I am, sitting on a bench,
minding my own business, my attention
riveted on the gleaming Hudson,
when the biggest bee I've ever seen,
reminiscent of the stubby Grumman
fighter plane of World War II,
nervily invades my space.

Since I'm not a flower, I'm not
all that nervous, but definitely prefer
the bee to conduct its manic, staccato
air show somewhere else,
in short, buzz off.

No sooner has that thought crossed
my mind than a second bee
shows up, and the two begin
a furious pas de deux.

Now here's the thing: for a fraction
of a second, they actually,
in mid-air,
make contact.

Clearly, it's way removed from
Whitman's dalliance of eagles,
"the twain...one...a moment's lull/
A motionless still balance in the air,"
but the respective metabolisms
are radically different, so isn't it possible,
in this totally improbable world,
that my two bees have pulled off
a quickie?

There's no time to contemplate
this question—a third bee has arrived
and the three weave a frenetic
vibrating cloud about my head—
the foreplay of a threesome?

Afraid of being stung, made victim
of a bee orgy, I gingerly get up
and go, leaving it
to a braver soul to serve
as the Kinsey of bees.

FINAL GALLOP

On J.M.W. Turner's *Death on a Pale Horse*

The painting makes you want to turn
it upside down, to get a better look at
Death's dangling head, on the verge of turning skull,
his carcass lying on its back athwart the horse's back,
skeleton arms flung out to the sides, the left one partly
cut off from view, the right one sporting an outsized
four-digit hand of bones. A curved ridge running
down Death's chest looks like
an exaggerated backbone—the horse itself
is not so much moving forward as rising.

The whole thing grips, repels, and makes
more sense than the Book of Revelation,
where Death rides the pale horse.
There's no rider here, only a sprawling, abandoned
bundle, being borne to God knows where.

AT THE MYKONOS ARCHEOLOGICAL MUSEUM

Rescued from a wilderness of ruin,
a wreck of rocks, a jumble of blocks
and broken statues, the exhibits here
have been given an orderly staging,
each assigned its place and placard,
each retaining a grace and elegance,
though barely so with the figure missing
its penis, replaced by a gaping, ragged hole.

ARRESTING SIGHT

Even if they could flash in unison,
not all the facets of all the diamonds
ever cut could match the brilliance
of the river's surface at this moment,
a coruscating sheet stretched from shore
to shore, water metamorphosed into points
of light so many, so shifting, as to mock
the notion of counting, this cornucopia of glittering
tossed our way by wind and sun, leaving
us unable to see a single reason
to look at anything else.

HELD

Sitting on the subway is a young woman
not of this century—no iPhone, no iPad,
no laptop, only a large tome held on her thighs,
from which, station after station, she never
lifts her gaze, willing prisoner of print.

I, in turn, gazing geezer, find the sight
of her perfect concentration riveting.
But here is my station and I must break
the spell. Getting up, I pause to lean down
and tell her "You make a beautiful reader."

Only then, smiling slightly,
does she raise her eyes.

AEOLUS IN APRIL

"Western wind, when wilt thou blow"
   —from anonymous 16th-century poem

Has anybody asked for this wind,
for this crazy late April day's chill gusts,
pure scions of March, bullying
their way across the river, pushing trees
around? Mighty winds are like Yahweh,
never allowing themselves to be directly visible,
but given over to showy manifestations instead,
like bringing down trees and power lines.
The Greeks quite properly assigned them to a god,
who shows up these days on occasion, like now,
which is more than Yahweh can say.

A KIND OF BOUQUET

for Gail

As I take this walk for my heart, I take in
members of the audience—daisies, chicory,
black-eyed Susan, Queen-Anne's–Lace—
rooted alongside the woodland path.

Shall I, to grace your table (as if it needed that),
make of the blameless blossoms a wild bouquet,
transporting them instantly from life to, for a while,
a pretty death, cluster of colors for you and your guests?

I stay my hand. Enough innocents are plucked
from their lives each day by a variety
of means, for a variety of ends. Please accept this,
instead, and simply imagine the real thing.

IRISES, OR, YOU NEVER KNOW

Erupting from spiky greens stalks,
come these explosions of inexplicable purple—
who could have dreamed such flowering?

Or that from our bodies, deaf, dumb,
and blind, should spring
our heads, so sensible?

Geysers thrust up out of plains,
mountains apex into flames.
O, blessed is our world,
that so rises in surprises

PASTORAL

Intent on maintaining the pace
of my semi-power walk,
I could easily have missed him,
off to the side as he was, and below me,
at the edge of the reservoir's steep bank,
standing still as the trees in the still air,
his line cast into the mirror-still water,
fixed in a perfect pastoral, waiting
for the advent of a hooked, thrashing fish,
wriggling for its life, a victim of stillness,
always an illusion in this poised world.

WHILE TAKING MY AEROBIC WALK IN THE RAIN

Fool toad, out in this downpour as am I,
intent on preserving your hide, as I my heart,
you take two lovely leaps away from me—
who would never do you harm—so swiftly
I see not you so much as the blurred arcs
of your circus stunts, those springs
charging me, as do the millions of drops
agitating the reservoir's surface,
all part of some great circuit
of energy, whose point may never come clear,
while always inviting us to leap in.

NOT YEATS'S TREE

"O chestnut- tree, great-rooted blossomer,
Are you the leaf, the blossom or the bole?"
—From "Among School Children"

Its trunk slightly corkscrewed in shape,
the papery bark of this silver birch
is interrupted at intervals by huge splotches
of dark, tortured-looking wood,
of greater circumference (if one could
measure such shapelessness) than that
of the trunk.

It is as though the tree had erupted
at these points, or been attacked
by some unimaginable monster
intent on perversely gnawing at the wood,
regurgitating rather than eating it.

Defying the scourge, the tree grows on,
refusing to ignore April's behest that it once
more dress itself in delicate leaves.

Which is "natural," the trunk's assailant,
or the greening branches?

DOWN ON ALL FOURS

March 21, 2003

Here I am, in my retirement, doing yet another chore.
Down on all fours on the high rear deck,
work gloves misplaced, I use my bare hands
to gather the dried leaves caught against
the netting nailed to the railing to prevent
the cat from committing inadvertent hara-kiri.
These crisp corpses I clutch are but a fraction
of what I saw brought down by autumn's natural catastrophe.

Dealt another card by the universe, I might
have been only twenty-five today, flying high,
five miles high over Baghdad, dropping my daisy-cutters.
It is good, good, to be down here
on all fours doing this grungy task,
cleaning up the premises, making them
ready for the entrance of a spring
dazed not only by the persistent cold,
but by the colored explosions leaking from the tube,
a mess I cannot contain, the leak
exhibiting our human staining of the world.

FOURTH OF JULY

Three compass points call for my gaze:
north, storm clouds gathering,
west, sun setting over the Hudson,
south, fireworks poised to begin.

The clouds are already part of a show,
dimmed strobe lights behind them alternating
with brilliant squiggles of naked lightning in front,
the whole thing silent, thunder too distant to be heard.

Sinking sun is making for the day
a beautiful death, mostly pale orange,
rendered paler in the reflecting water,
the glorious light draining subtly away.

Nothing silent or subtle about the fireworks,
the showiest thing we do, and among the most
endearing, separating noise and explosions
from destruction, keeping them more related to birth—
so many begin their ascent looking like
gigantic, wriggling sperm cells, transforming
into sudden huge blossoms of light,
to which we can only say "Ah" and "Ah."

LAST BUDS

Gallant azalea, you on your last legs,
putting forth a grand total of nine buds
when you should be teeming with them—
and those pathetic few a miracle,
since, sapless, almost all of you now
is but a cluster of stark stems—
gallant azalea, you must go, sacrificed
to stern aesthetics, the need to have
the space you occupy greet the eye
with a quota of color you're not meeting.

So, equipped with fork and spade,
I dig methodically all around you,
periodically giving you a sharp tug,
which, to your credit, you resist.
But at last you part with stepmother earth,
held briefly now only by my alien hands,
before being tossed out of the garden.

(Nearing my end, will I resist to the last,
will I be showing any buds at all?)

Today I spot you at the edge
of the woods where I'd thrown you.
Your buds are now blossoms—
you are breaking my heart.

LATE AFTERNOON
ON THE BANKS OF THE HUDSON

The sun has laid down a path,
a blurry, shimmering, flowing
surface brilliantly corrugated—
I could drink this in for hours,
but the sun, however slowly,
is turning down its rheostat,
ruthless, ready as ever to turn
everything to darkness, rebuking
the upstart river, claiming for itself
the right to symbolize passing time.

EMERGENCE

She apparently was not out for a swim
in the lake crib, but content simply
to bob indefinitely, smiling, up to her neck
in the water. She stayed and stayed.
When, finally, she emerged, huge thighs and legs
came into view, shocking folds of flesh,
more appropriate to some great prehistoric amphibian
than a human being. The smile was gone.
She must have known how she would strike viewers,
wanted to stay concealed as long as possible,
to pass for just another one of us, experiencing
the buoyancy of immersion with special relish,
connecting with the watery origin of us all,
postponing as long as possible her necessary
coming out, her taking up the inescapable burden
of being her particular self.

LOVE THY NEIGHBOR

I

From below this morning's headline
nailing a local nanny for abusing her charges,
the lady's name floats up to fill the eye.
She is our nearest and best neighbor,
large, ungainly, silver-white-haired,
lover of chamber music,
ballsy uprooter of poison ivy,
planter of bulbs and annuals,
tireless transplanter of pachysandra,
her farming girlhood transmuted
into a mania for gardening.
The anemone that bloomed in our living room some weeks back,
the fountaining spray of forsythia in our kitchen now,
her gifts.
She was caught on videotape smacking an eleven-month-old,
tossing it onto a floor pillow, saying Wheeeee, kicking it,
then throwing a bottle at the head of a ten-month-old.

II

This morning, below our feeder,
a visitation—three ungainly beings,
gross round bodies supporting little, ugly, reddish heads,
have waddled over from the nanny's driveway,
and peck and peck and peck at everything in sight.
If the finches bringing the daily gift of their yellow-jeweled bodies
to our feeder are birds, can these be birds as well?

III

What a species!
Love thy neighbor? Be my guest.
For me, for now, this will have to do.

BIRTH-MONTH

September, birth-month, won't you ever
make up your mind as to what you are?
First you give us Labor Day, celebrating
work by having us desist from it, then
you come up with the first day of fall,
almost always in a stretch of summery weather,
belied by diminishing light—
you are the year's Limbo, the very feel
of your air cloying, its soft
ambiguity vaguely irritating.

Still, you and I are a good fit these days,
anomaly that I am, my own September,
still open to the pull of youth, of beauty,
even as I go down to wrinkle and ache,
more expressive than ever, more feeling,
even as I go from room to empty room.

Still, if you come, oh September,
can October be far behind?

AGAINST YOM KIPPUR

Yom Kippur: a Jewish holiday
incorporating a prayer during which
the worshiper beats his chest
repeatedly, while reciting the list of sins
committed during the previous year.

Today, this wishy-washy
September has converted to clarity.
Everything is brilliantly what it is.
Misery lifts. A thrilling blue
glows over a world so perfect
no one need atone, no one need
go indoors to beat at a heart
beating in sweet thankfulness.

HOMAGE

Have you ever seen a squirrel
strolling? Well, neither have I.
It's not in their repertoire.
Freezing is, which they sometimes
stupidly do as a car approaches.
There's also loping, or scampering,
their tails undulating in a series
of lovely sine curves—do those
have a function, or are they simply
an aesthetic dividend tossed off
in the course of evolution
by an absent-minded, prodigious
Nature? We'll never know.

Be that as it may, there is also the matter
of squirrel acrobatics, their prodigious feats
on trees, or poles or clothes-lines supporting
bird-feeders, which they seem to take
as having been put out expressly for them.
These performances may not be quite up
to the Frenchman who traversed a tight-
rope strung high between the twin towers,
but they'll do, none being a one-time
publicity stunt, but a daily task,
a risk matter-of-factly taken on,
which links squirrels, I suppose,
to those firemen who rushed in
to the towering pyres.

JAPANESE MAPLE AT MY WINDOW

No, you are not Frost's tree,
you do not reflect my life
nor anything else except the light.
You are simply yourself
as you do a serene slow burn
through these gradually
shortening days,
or, to put it differently,
as you exchange nondescript green
for scarlet, thus decked out to meet
death in a killer dress.
You are not a symbol of anything,
but rather, a model, going to your end
luminous, the rheostat of autumn
turning you up, up,
as the diminishing light winds down,
you beautiful, beautiful lady in red.

HERDING LEAVES

The last round-up for these critters,
you could say—thousands of them
mixed in with hundreds of acorns,
death and potential new life
all scrambled together in fall's motley,
the whole kit and caboodle fleeing, panicked,
in the face of the directed whirlwind kicked up
by my bright-red leaf-blower, artfully cutting
off their retreat, driving them into cowed piles,
to be raked onto a tarp, dragged off to the entropy
of the nearby woods, which have seen all this before.

NOT ON ANYBODY'S SHOPPING LIST

Weeks before Halloween, a false
but life-size human skull has appeared
on the checkout counter of the local market.
Who was in such a rush to deliver
this jolt to the captive customers?

Undeniable is the power of a skull
to appall—its usual high cheekbones,
so often an attribute of beautiful women,
but now released from beneath the skin,
are only good for jutting out and into your brain.
And is that a grin or a grimace we are seeing?
Does a skull proclaim the sure victory of death,
or the pain of having been stripped of its face?

The momento mori had its place in the age
of belief. What is it doing here?

HALLOWEEN PARADE

Here they come, kids, adults, even dogs,
marching raggedly down Main Street, celebrating
make-believe in a potpourri of costumes,
the bands' trumpets and trombones
giving their all, drums rapping out tight,
compelling rhythms, spectators clapping
in unison, all joined in a one-night
community of joy.

Leading the parade, a man in black,
riding a black horse, his face
invisible beneath a black cloth—
bringing up the rear, fire engines,
sirens at full strength as if for a real conflagration.

The whole spectacle a fusion of paraders
and onlookers, of freedom and order,
play and discipline, unintentionally
showing itself contained by those great
possibilities of death and disaster.

GARDENING IN LATE FALL

Ballsy pansy,
November survivor,
bowed but still brilliant,
I pluck you and press you.

In the later and darker,
your velvet embers,
purple and yellow,
will glow a reminder,
momento vitae.

DOWNCAST

Flattened, fastened to the asphalt by moisture,
deprived of all fall flamboyance, leaves cast off
by once mothering trees lack the appeal to ask
walkers and joggers not to tread upon them.

Where will they go? The man-made ground
has no inclination to give them burial, as would the earth,
however slowly. Drying winds will toss them about
before disappearing them in obliteration's helter skelter,
where they will rest, awaiting us.

AGAINST FALL

All the leaves are down,
but no California dreamin' for me,
rather, Connecticut raking,
a summoning of the will
against the trees' shameless
abandonment of their shriveled charges,
the new shag rug swamping
driveway, walkway, lawn, garden,
the forms and boundaries that help
us withstand our swirling world.

So, I will take arms—blower, rake, tarp—
against a sea of leaves—thwarting
the obliterations this season would bring,
knowing the ultimate blotting out
is down the road somewhere, waiting.

OLD MAN RIVER

Rewarding its weekly winding,
the antique German clock gives forth
its tick, its tock, as if echoing
a small, nameless tool working its will
on the span of my life, of yours.

When was it we fell into time,
that is, the measuring of it,
standing on its banks,
segmenting its streaming,
instead of simply floating on its current,
like Huck and Jim on the Mississippi?

FIRE-WATCH

Fluted white wood and delicate-pink marble
help compose the fireplace surround.
Nothing composes the fire, its flames
jagged, frenzied, leaping, eating
its source, jaws occasionally snapping.
It can even bite us if we get careless,
but how much pleasure we take in this
pet version of the real thing. Out in the dark
forests of the far West, set loose
by lightning or simply by some idiot,
fire comes as engulfer, manic destroyer,
ingesting in hours the slow growths
of centuries. Even there we humans are lucky,
still protected by the cocoon of light-years
from the cosmic variety, stars flaming
themselves to death in conflagrations
that make the greatest forest holocaust
seem but the sprayings of a sparkler.
Thank you, all you deep space.
I think I'll put another log on.

AGAINST FROST

There was nothing wrong in his having stopped.
But he should have gotten down,
turned his back on the querulous horse,
and, moving over the snow, listened
to the down compacting under his boots,
the one dominant sound in a world turned white mute.
He should have thrust out his tongue
to take in the flaky manna, and been falling
not for the dark of the woods, but the light,
the light, sifting from sky to glimmering ground,
losing his way with each lovely step.

GIFT HORSE

A rainbow here? In a parking lot?
Now? In this fading light of a December day,
wet snow falling? Yes, of a sort,
thanks to a huge oil stain, dripped
product of some departed vehicle,
converted now to a radiant melange
of iridescent color, unintended gift
of a defective engine and neglectful
driver—let's take what we can get
as we pass through this imperfect world.

ALL EARS

There is only one way to listen
to music—alone, at night, the volume
turned way up in your vehicle
as you glide along dark country roads,
tuned into the sweet power
of Pavaroti's tenor, the not quite
sung, sly songs of Leonard Cohen,
the honey pouring from Paul Desmond's sax,
your whole being now all ears,
taking in, over the engine's hum,
these variegated musics of the spheres

LEVITATED

LBJ's lifting his poor pooch by the ears
was one thing, my being so lifted, even
as my fingers remain firmly curled around
the steering wheel, is quite another,
my head now suspended somewhere well
above the highway, the result of driving
to the accompaniment of a Callas CD.

Her delicate negotiation of ladders
of notes, ascending or descending,
her daring high fortissimos just this
side of shrieks, embody a total
commitment to her roles. Life does not
give many of us the grand passions
of opera, but here they are, entered
into me, and I hover above this world,
pierced by arrowy notes, slain but more
alive than ever, as I speed, sobbing,
sobbing, down the empty road.

YOU NEVER KNOW

I had given up on this favorite path
planting the seeds of any more poems,
when I spotted a young man coasting
towards me on roller blades, being
drawn by the three small dogs
running at full tilt before him, as he held
their leashes in one hand, while cradling
a tiny pooch in the other. I stepped
aside to give room to this impromptu
circus act, this comic equivalent
of a Roman charioteer, thinking
one should not give up on our old earth
bringing off something new, and
as he passed, I said to him "Thank you.

DECEMBER RAIN

Incomparably dreary, yet this truncated
day of heavy winds and driving rain,
has yielded up, in its last hour,
a small, light-blue sky window
under a stretch of salmon cloud fast-yielding
to the darkening surround, and I have found,
if not the thing itself, an emblem of hope,
frail, brief, but hope, snatched from the jaws
of gloom, and I can only give thanks
for this late-bloomer.

VIVA HEISENBERG

Anything could come of this hodgepodge
of a sky—a continuation of the afternoon's
premature darkening, a knitting together
of the blue patches, thereby undoing
the thunder-storm forecast,
those storms for real, or a last-minute
emergence of the sun from under the clouds,
casting its klieg-light on the world.

Nobody knows for sure—forecasts are but
educated guesses. This is as it should be.
Let our universe always stay well
beyond the nets of our knowledge, let
uncertainty prevail, let there not be
such a thing as a sure thing, at least not
in large matters, such as this sky
trying to make up its cloudy mind.

A NAME THAT WILL ENDURE

No, this is not a mistake on your part or mine,
you are reading me correctly.
A Shakespeare contemporary, one Thomas Bastard,
is included in The Oxford Book of Short Poems ,
another of those navy-blue, gold-stamped volumes
issued by Oxford University Press, whose quiet elegance
exudes authority and permanence.

True, Bastard's is a charming piece,
about the quality of young children's speech,
which he sees as crucially, sweetly, conditioned
by toothlessness—clearly, a fresh, original work.

Still, here am I, straining to get my poems
published in such places
as The Hairy Centipede Review,
or The Quasimodo Quarterly, knowing
full well my name is destined only for oblivion,
while this guy, with that moniker,
sits forever ensconced in Poet's Heaven,
which is to say, on library shelves everywhere.
What nerve—what a bastard.

KING OF THE ROAD

Vaguely irritated by its insistent wail,
imperious, flashy king of the road,
I pull over to let the ambulance pass.
As I watch it go by, something in me
drops. This is happening in Danbury,
but the name on the ambulance reads
Redding, my little town. Do I know
the person inside? Will there come a time
when my counterpart pulls over
to make way for me on my royal ride
to Danbury General Hospital, atop a throne
that anyone would gladly abdicate?

ZSA ZSA

Fixed at the bottom of the TV screen,
the words: "Zsa Zsa Gabor has leg
amputated." I can take in nothing else,

though she hasn't been a presence for decades.
Most known for her many marriages
(eventually numbering nine), a fixture

on late-night talk shows, exuding
a Hungarian-tinted babble, she had floated
away, intact, into the limbo of the formerly

famous, crowded out by the hordes
of newer celebrities, though the years
brought slivers of attention (through

marrying a prince, or accusing a daughter
of forgery), but also what they might
have brought to anybody—a car crash,

a stroke, a blocked artery. Now this,
a severed leg, the lingering image
of frothy, blond perfection replaced

by the gravitas of great age (93!),
and amputation.

WHO KNOWS WHERE A WALK WILL LEAD?

It's crunch time out here, I mean literally,
if, like me, you are walking through the fallen
leaves and acorns of Kingsland Point Park,
wondering if, by stepping on the acorns,
you are increasing their chances of rooting
in the earth and becoming—surely a miracle—
oaks themselves, or are inflicting irreparable damage
on them, joining them to the detritus of the world.

In short, for a short time anyway, you may have become
something of a god, determining life or death,
even as you try to fight your own mortality by taking
one of your power walks.

I don't want an answer to the question posed
in stanza one. Let the trodden acorns
take their place beside Schrödinger's cat,
which, in his famous thought experiment,
could be both dead and alive (do not ask me
to explain that—go Google it if you're interested).

Just allow me to finish my walk.

WHAT ARE THE CHANCES?

Striding along in my Gravity Defyers
(sneakers, that is), I crunch, at every step,
countless numbers of acorns cast down
by the stands of oaks in Kingsland Point Park,
knowing that few of these will succeed
in the burial and resurrection needed
for new oaks—perhaps none will,
a possibility rendering the whole plethora
pointless. You could say the same for all
those squiggly human sperm cells striving
to reach an egg, the chances for any given one
next to nothing, new life coming into being
at all only because the scheme of things employs
a cast of millions to keep the show going.

Wasn't this principle written into the universe
from the very first, the Big Bang birthing
stars whose numbers we neatly designate—10^{24}—
but cannot imagine—mind-boggling quantities
resulting in our lonely, life-bearing planet,
and perhaps no others?

Time to end my excursion into the park
and universe—this improbable being
is heading home for a nap.

WHISTLE WHILE YOU WALK

Sooner or later on my woodland walks,
I find myself whistling, almost always
something from the American Songbook,
and I wonder whether the notes I propel
upon the air, those invisible bubbles,
are having any effect on my surroundings,
whether the trees are perking up their leaves,
whether the birds are intrigued by melodies
more elaborate than their own, whether
the fish in the adjoining reservoir are breaking
the surface, the better to hear Gershwin or Porter,
as this local boy turns Orpheus wannabe.

TO THE PUPILS OF MY EYES

How do your tiny, twin portals admit
these giant, cotton-candy clouds,
set in the immensity of sky's dome?

How do the blind manage unalloyed darkness,
since life is so inseparable from seeing?

At my death, you will contract dramatically,
your one-time, generous gateways turning
into reverse black holes, admitting nothing.

WHAT DESIGN?

"What brought the kindred spider to that height?"
—From Frost's "Design"

Oh, come on—I can't take a shower
without having to see this thing,
a spider clinging to the back of
the soap-holder? What brought
the spider to that height? Nothing
that is bringing it a moth or
any other munchy by the looks
of things. But maybe something brought
me, to spot the spider, to note
its perch as pointless, to wonder if
either of us will find sustenance
by spinning what we do from our
innards, and then simply waiting.

OTHER ANAPHORA LITERARY PRESS TITLES

Film Theory and Modern Art
Editor: Anna Faktorovich

Interview with Larry Niven
Editor: Anna Faktorovich

Dragonflies in the Cowburbs
Donelle Dreese

Domestic Subversive
Roberta Salper

Radical Agrarian Economics
Anna Faktorovich

Fajitas and Beer Convention
Roger Rodriguez

Spirit of Tabasco
Richard Diedrichs

Skating in Concord
Jean LeBlanc

CPSIA information can be obtained
at www.ICGtesting.com
Printed in the USA
FFOW02n0535271015
17957FF